SNAKES
LOOK-AND-LEARN
by
W.P. MARA

LIST OF PHOTOGRAPHERS

The following is a list of the photographers whose work appears in this book: C. Banks, R. D. Bartlett, Paul Freed, G. Pisani, A. Kerstitch, Dr. Sherman. A. Minton, Roberta Kayne, Jim Merli, K. H. Switak, B. Kahl, W. P. Mara, P. J. Stafford, Guido Dingerkus, Kenneth T. Nemuras, Ken Lucas, A. t. Hun, S. Kochetov, Robert T. Zappalorti, Ron Everhart, A. v. d. Nieuwenhuizen, Robert S. Simmons, John Iverson, W. Wuster, John Visser, Jeff Wines, William B. Allen, Jr., G. Marcuse, S. B. Reichling, J. T. Kellnhauser, M. J. Cox, H. Hansen, J. K. Langhammer, R. G. Markel, J. Gee, R. A. Winstel, Ludwig Trutnau, and Dr. Warren E. Burgess.

Cover photograph of a juvenile albino Corn Snake, *Elaphe guttata guttata*, by J. Visser

© Copyright 1993 by T.F.H. Publications

Distributed in the UNITED STATES to the Pet Trade by T.F.H. Publications, Inc., One T.F.H. Plaza, Neptune City, NJ 07753; distributed in the UNITED STATES to the Bookstore and Library Trade by National Book Network, Inc. 4720 Boston Way, Lanham MD 20706; in CANADA to the Pet Trade by H & L Pet Supplies Inc., 27 Kingston Crescent, Kitchener, Ontario N2B 2T6; Rolf C. Hagen Ltd., 3225 Sartelon Street, Montreal 382 Quebec; in CANADA to the Book Trade by Macmillan of Canada (A Division of Canada Publishing Corporation), 164 Commander Boulevard, Agincourt, Ontario M1S 3C7; in the United Kingdom by T.F.H. Publications, PO Box 15, Waterlooville PO7 6BQ; in AUSTRALIA AND THE SOUTH PACIFIC by T.F.H. (Australia), Pty. Ltd., Box 149, Brookvale 2100 N.S.W., Australia; in NEW ZEALAND by Brooklands Aquarium Ltd. 5 McGiven Drive, New Plymouth, RD1 New Zealand; in Japan by T.F.H. Publications, Japan—Jiro Tsuda, 10-12-3 Ohjidai, Sakura, Chiba 285, Japan; in SOUTH AFRICA by Multipet Pty. Ltd., P.O. Box 35347, Northway, 4065, South Africa. Published by T.F.H. Publications, Inc.

Manufactured in the United States of America by T.F.H. Publications, Inc.

SUGGESTED READING

TS-166, 192 pgs, 175+ photos

KW-132, 96 pgs, 40+ photos

KW-002, 96 pgs, 70+ photos

TS-154, 192 pgs, 175+ photos

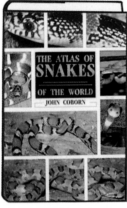
TS-128, 592 pgs, 1400+ photos

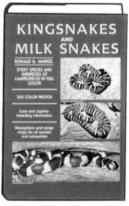
TS-125, 144 pgs, 200+ photos

TS-145, 288 pgs, 280+ photos

T-112, 64 pgs, 40+ photos

KW-127, 96 pgs, 80+ photos

PS-316, 128 pgs, 50+ photos

KW-196, 128 pgs, 100+ photos

PS-769, 189 pgs, 50+ photos

SK-017, 64 pgs, 40+ photos

YF-115, 36 pgs, 20+ photos

PS-311, 96 pgs, 45+ photos

SK-015, 64 pgs, 35+ photos

These and thousands of other animal books have been published by TFH. TFH is the world's largest publisher of animal books. You can find our titles at the same place you bought this one, or write to us for a free catalog.

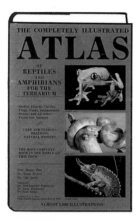

H-1102, 830 pgs, 1800+ photos

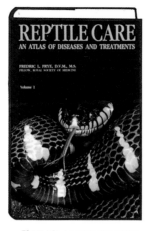

TS-165, VOL. I, 655 pgs, 1850+ photos

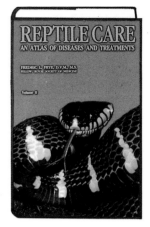

TS-165, VOL. II, 655 pgs, 1850+ photos

PS-207, 230 pgs, B&W illus.

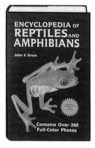

H-935, 576 pgs, 260+ photos

PS-876, 384 pgs, 175+ photos

KW-197, 128 pgs, 110+ photos

TW-115, 256 pgs, 180+ photos

CO-0438, 96 pgs, 80+ photos

TU-023, 64 pgs, 50+ photos

PB-126, 64 pgs, 32+ photos

AP-925, 160 pgs, 120+ photos

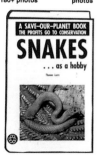

TT-001, 96 pgs, 80+ photos

J-007, 48 pgs, 25+ photos

TU-015, 64 pgs, 50+ photos

TW-111, 256 pgs, 180+ photos

These and thousands of other animal books have been published by TFH. TFH is the world's largest publisher of animal books. You can find our titles at the same place you bought this one, or write to us for a free catalog.

INTRODUCTION

Snakes are fascinating creatures. They are not slimy, contrary to the belief of many, nor are they aggressive toward humans (in fact, they would rather avoid a human than attack one). There have been so many horribly unfair certitudes tailored around these magnificent creatures that it sometimes amazes me there's a hobby concerning them at all! Snakes are graceful, attractive, alert, in some cases fairly intelligent, and in many ways highly beneficial to the world around us, but here is not the place to say all this.
Read on and find out for yourself just how wonderful they are.

◀ Snakes have intrigued man for centuries, inspiring artists from the past to capture their images forever. This is a great monument to the fact that even if people feel revulsion toward snakes, the are still captivated by them at the same time.

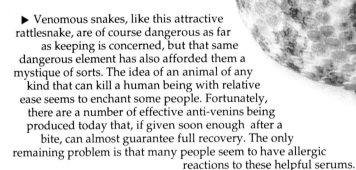

▶ Venomous snakes, like this attractive rattlesnake, are of course dangerous as far as keeping is concerned, but that same dangerous element has also afforded them a mystique of sorts. The idea of an animal of any kind that can kill a human being with relative ease seems to enchant some people. Fortunately, there are a number of effective anti-venins being produced today that, if given soon enough after a bite, can almost guarantee full recovery. The only remaining problem is that many people seem to have allergic reactions to these helpful serums.

◀ Photo of a snake body, stained to show different regions. This type of activity is commonplace in the many branches of science that concern snakes and tells many useful things about the animal's biology. In fact, there are quite a few things one can do with a deceased snake, including stuffing the body and displaying it, stripping it down to the skeleton and displaying that or collecting specimens in jars of formalin or alcohol.

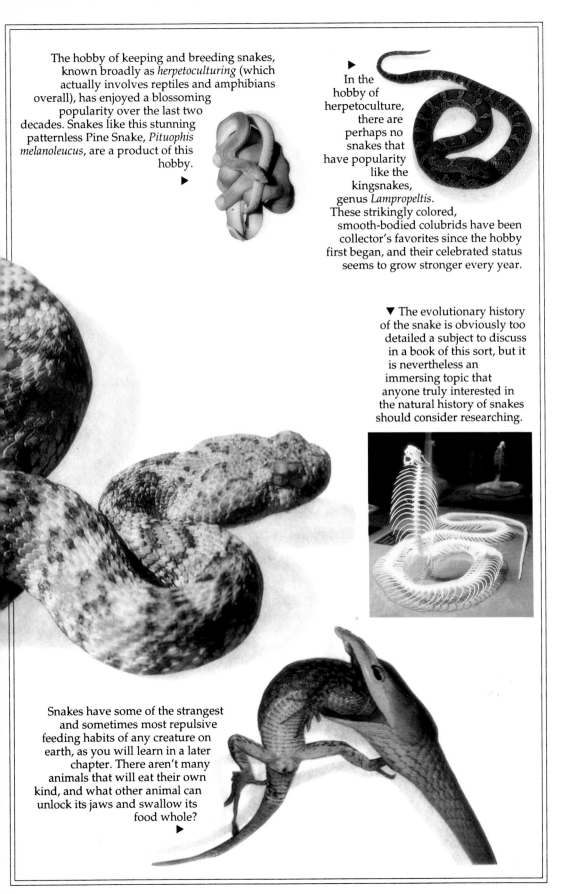

The hobby of keeping and breeding snakes, known broadly as *herpetoculturing* (which actually involves reptiles and amphibians overall), has enjoyed a blossoming popularity over the last two decades. Snakes like this stunning patternless Pine Snake, *Pituophis melanoleucus*, are a product of this hobby.
▶

▶
In the hobby of herpetoculture, there are perhaps no snakes that have popularity like the kingsnakes, genus *Lampropeltis*. These strikingly colored, smooth-bodied colubrids have been collector's favorites since the hobby first began, and their celebrated status seems to grow stronger every year.

▼ The evolutionary history of the snake is obviously too detailed a subject to discuss in a book of this sort, but it is nevertheless an immersing topic that anyone truly interested in the natural history of snakes should consider researching.

Snakes have some of the strangest and sometimes most repulsive feeding habits of any creature on earth, as you will learn in a later chapter. There aren't many animals that will eat their own kind, and what other animal can unlock its jaws and swallow its food whole?
▶

HOW SNAKES EAT

Unlike other animals, snakes have a remarkable feature that allows them to swallow prey items much larger than the size of their mouths: their jaws unlock! This enables a small garter snake to take down a giant frog, or a kingsnake to eat a huge rat. Some pythons have even been known to swallow whole tigers! The bones in their skulls are loosely connected by various muscles and ligaments rather than constructed as one solid structure. Thus, when something large passes through their mouths, everything stretches apart. There is of course a limit to just how far this stretching can go, but you'd be amazed some of the things a snake can swallow.

▲ It's not surprising to learn that snakes will feed off the creatures that live in the natural environment around them. This Ribbon Snake, *Thamnophis sauritus*, for example, never strays far from water, so naturally it will include frogs in its diet.

▶ Mice are one of the most popular snake foods. They are accepted by a wide variety of species and can be obtained either in pet stores or by breeding them yourself.

While newborn snakes already have acute squeezing instincts, their tiny bodies often are not developed enough to constrict with any great efficiency. Their movements will be jerky and awkward, but they will get the job done nevertheless. ▶

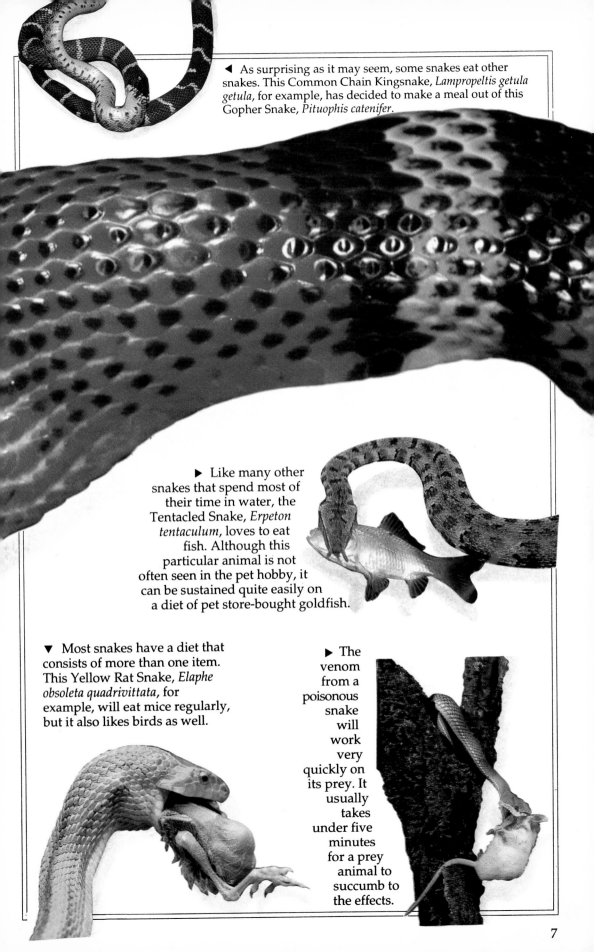

◄ As surprising as it may seem, some snakes eat other snakes. This Common Chain Kingsnake, *Lampropeltis getula getula*, for example, has decided to make a meal out of this Gopher Snake, *Pituophis catenifer*.

► Like many other snakes that spend most of their time in water, the Tentacled Snake, *Erpeton tentaculum*, loves to eat fish. Although this particular animal is not often seen in the pet hobby, it can be sustained quite easily on a diet of pet store-bought goldfish.

▼ Most snakes have a diet that consists of more than one item. This Yellow Rat Snake, *Elaphe obsoleta quadrivittata*, for example, will eat mice regularly, but it also likes birds as well.

► The venom from a poisonous snake will work very quickly on its prey. It usually takes under five minutes for a prey animal to succumb to the effects.

WHAT SNAKES EAT

The keeper of snakes is indeed lucky, for most snakes have a highly varied diet. Depending on the exact species you have, you may find yourself supplying your pets with mice, rats, frogs, toads, lizards, crickets, earthworms, goldfish, and maybe even reptile eggs! These food items can be acquired from a number of places, but the simplest and most logical would be at your local pet store. Virtually every store that sells snakes will sell mice, rats, crickets and goldfish. There are also a number of private breeders who provide the same. As far as frogs, toads, lizards, reptile eggs, and earthworms are concerned, you will probably have to go out and find these things yourself.

▲ The hunter and the hunted. Moments after this photo was taken, the Tentacled Snake, *Erpeton tentaculum*, grabbed and swallowed its prey. Fish make up a small percentage of the overall ophidian diet, but those species that eat fish usually don't take much else.

▲ A snake eating a fellow reptile? May sound strange, but it certainly happens. In fact, there are quite a large number of species that do this. Kingsnakes, for example, are notorious reptile-eaters, especially other snakes. Here we see a Common Chain Kingsnake, *Lampropeltis getula getula*, swallowing an Eastern Glass Lizard, *Ophisaurus ventralis*.

▶ There aren't too many snakes which specialize in egg-eating, but there are a few. Some of them take bird eggs, some take fish eggs (sea snakes), and some even eat the eggs of other reptiles. This African Egg-eater, *Dasypeltis* sp., really has to stretch in order to take down this meal.

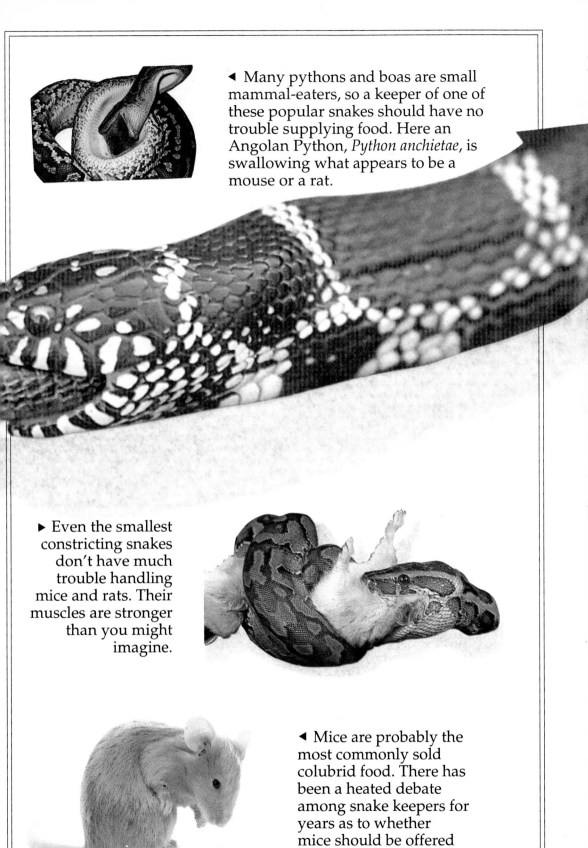

◄ Many pythons and boas are small mammal-eaters, so a keeper of one of these popular snakes should have no trouble supplying food. Here an Angolan Python, *Python anchietae*, is swallowing what appears to be a mouse or a rat.

▶ Even the smallest constricting snakes don't have much trouble handling mice and rats. Their muscles are stronger than you might imagine.

◄ Mice are probably the most commonly sold colubrid food. There has been a heated debate among snake keepers for years as to whether mice should be offered alive or dead.

REPRODUCTION

Perhaps the most fascinating aspect of the snake—surely one of the most often studied—is its reproduction. Both scientists and hobbyists alike have dedicated hundreds and thousands of pages to the recording of data concerning this most interesting part of their biology. Some of the more intriguing details include male combat rituals, the male's habit of "biting" the female's neck during copulation, and the frequently underestimated maternal instinct some females show toward their eggs and/or young. It would be an understatement to say captive-breeding has become a wondrous hobby all its own and may be the only key to the ultimate preservation of many species.

Rat snakes are among the most often captive-bred serpents. In this stunning photo you see a clutch of Stripe-tailed Rat Snake, *Elaphe taeniura*, eggs as they hatch. The young will slit through the leathery shells with the aid of an "egg tooth" which will fall off shortly thereafter and never grow back.
▶

In the wild, snake eggs can be found in any number of places. Some snakes will lay them deep in subterranean burrows, others will crawl under fallen and decaying logs, and then there are those snakes that dig into moist leaf piles. There are of course other places as well, but the common denominator is moisture. ▼

▶
A keeper may notice that newly-hatched snakes still have an umbilical cord attached to their bellies that run back into the eggs. The temptation to simply cut these cords is natural, but not advisable. The snake could be killed.

◀ Watching a mother snake lay her eggs is a fascinating sight, but even if you are lucky enough to be around when this happens, it should be remembered that the snake will be going through enough stress just trying to lay and does not need any added distractions.

▲

The North American Copperheads, *Agkistrodon contortrix*, have a particularly graceful male combat ritual in which two males will wrap around one another and try to "pin" the other to the ground. There are usually no truly violent actions taken by either party, and thus neither snake gets injured. The winner of course is the one that gets to mate with the female.

▶

A useful tool for all snake breeders is the sexing probe. It is nothing more than a pencil-sized steel rod with a tiny ball at the tip. When coated with an inert jelly, it can be inserted into the cloaca (left or right side, not the middle) and gently pushed toward the tail. If the probe is blocked after three or four scales, the animal is probably a female. If it runs more than five, it is probably a male.

▶ If you think a snake will simply slide out of its egg right after it's born you are mistaken. Some snakes have been known to remain in these tiny encasements for days. It is important for a breeder to know that a newborn snake will do this if it senses danger so it should not be disturbed. Let the animal come out voluntarily.

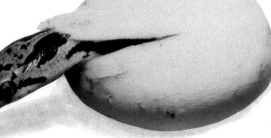

PATTERNS OF SNAKES

No one could argue the point that one of the most appealing aspects of snakes is their seemingly infinite variety of colors and patterns. Patterning is important to field herpetologists for identification, although not wholly reliable, and to the snakes themselves for a number of reasons, including defense, offense (when necessary), and perhaps most importantly, to blend into their background creating an effective camouflage (although some snakes seem to defy this theory by having colors which distinctly stand out against the more somber tones of their environment).

► It wouldn't be hard to guess why this type of pattern is referred to as "lined." Most lined snakes have not one, but a series of lines that run parallel on either side of the vertebrae. Most of these species have at least two lines and some have as many as six or eight, but a few, like this California Kingsnake, *Lampropeltis getula californiae*, have just the one.

▲ The definition of a "ringed" pattern is obvious—rings are markings encircling a snake's body entirely, and this includes running across the belly. Many snakes have the Latin name "annulata" which literally means ringed. Many of the tri-colored kingsnakes and Milk Snakes are annulated.

Speckled patterns are usually messy and consequently not very attractive, but some speckled snakes have a neat, orderly arrangement to their speckling and the effect is visually pleasing. Shown here is the Speckled Racer, *Drymobius margaritiferus.* ▼

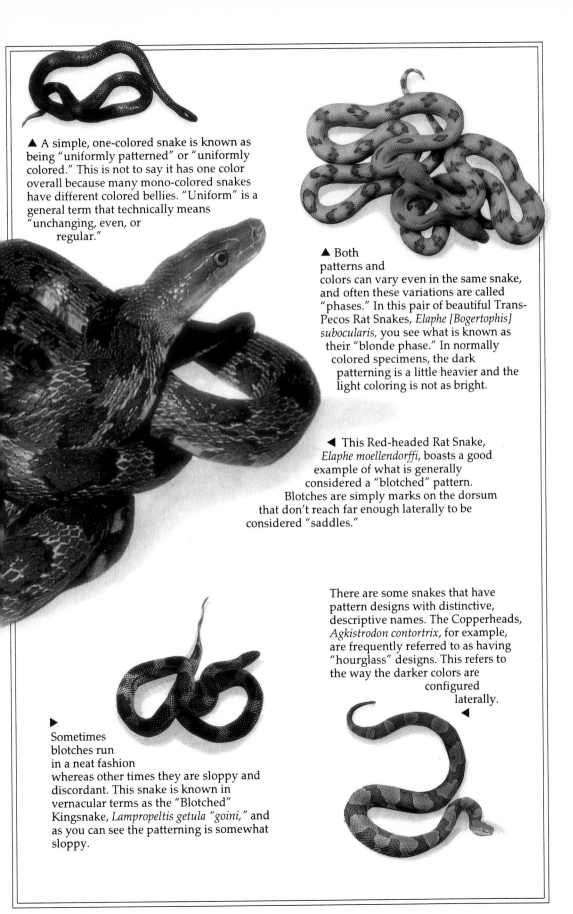

▲ A simple, one-colored snake is known as being "uniformly patterned" or "uniformly colored." This is not to say it has one color overall because many mono-colored snakes have different colored bellies. "Uniform" is a general term that technically means "unchanging, even, or regular."

▲ Both patterns and colors can vary even in the same snake, and often these variations are called "phases." In this pair of beautiful Trans-Pecos Rat Snakes, *Elaphe [Bogertophis] subocularis,* you see what is known as their "blonde phase." In normally colored specimens, the dark patterning is a little heavier and the light coloring is not as bright.

◄ This Red-headed Rat Snake, *Elaphe moellendorffi,* boasts a good example of what is generally considered a "blotched" pattern. Blotches are simply marks on the dorsum that don't reach far enough laterally to be considered "saddles."

There are some snakes that have pattern designs with distinctive, descriptive names. The Copperheads, *Agkistrodon contortrix,* for example, are frequently referred to as having "hourglass" designs. This refers to the way the darker colors are configured laterally.

► Sometimes blotches run in a neat fashion whereas other times they are sloppy and discordant. This snake is known in vernacular terms as the "Blotched" Kingsnake, *Lampropeltis getula "goini,"* and as you can see the patterning is somewhat sloppy.

◄

WHAT'S IN A NAME?

The study of a snake's name, both English and Latin, is a fascinating activity that can tell you much about the snake in question. The study of words in general is called *etymology* and can open many doors in a language that otherwise seems senseless and illogical. Once you start getting a grasp on why certain snakes are called what they're called it will be easier to understand other aspects of their life history. Also, many of the seemingly trivial bits of information unearthed through this study may lead your interests on to further curiosities. The problem with the Latin classifications of so many animals is that the words mean nothing to most people and consequently they become disinterested in them. But these words do in fact have meanings and if you take the time to study them you may find them much more intriguing than originally thought.

Sometimes a name can be tricky and even misleading, so an interested person must always be thorough in his or her research. The Racers of North America, for example, have the species name *constrictor*, and one would easily assume that this is based on the way they kill their prey. In truth, however, racers do not constrict at all. ▼

►

Sometimes a snake's genus name will be based simply on its location. The Glossy Snakes, for example, belong to the monotypic (containing only one species) genus *Arizona*, which, beyond being a state in the USA where they occur, also means "an arid area." The specimen shown is *Arizona elegans philipi*, the Painted Desert Glossy Snake.

▲ Noted figures in the scientific world are often the focus of a species or subspecies name. The Northern Scarlet Snake is known in Latin as *Cemophora coccinea copei*, the tertiary name being inspired by naturalist Edward Drinker Cope.

The tiny little Brown Snake, *Storeria dekayi*, is also known as DeKay's Snake and is named for noted 19th century New York naturalist James Edward DeKay. There are a number of subspecies involved as well, each with their own stories. One, *S. d. wrightorum*, was named after Albert Hazen and Anna Allen Wright, authors of the well-known *Handbook of Snakes*. ▼

◄ Sometimes a snake's common name is inspired by something obvious. The Ringneck Snake, *Diadophis punctatus*, shown here, is a good example of this. Other telltale names include the Green Snake, the Snail-eating Snake, and the Black-headed Snake.

Sometimes, although rarely, an entire genus will be named after a figure in the scientific world. One of these rare exceptions is the Trans-Pecos Rat Snake, which is occasionally placed in the genus *Bogertophis*, named for late herpetologist Charles M. Bogert. ▼

▲

Sometimes names will change over the course of time, and this rule applies to English names as well as Latin ones. The snake we know today as the Yellow Rat Snake, *Elaphe obsoleta quadrivittata*, was at one time better known as the Chicken Snake, a named earned from its habit of raiding chicken coops for food.

MIMICRY

There are two generally accepted types of mimicry: Batesian and Mullerian, obviously based on theories formulated by persons with those names (Bates and Muller). The former, the Batesian theory, was outlined in 1861 and is the one we will be applying here. It states, in loose terms, that an animal (non-dangerous) will copy, in appearance, a model (dangerous) in the hopes of warding off a predator that is already aware of the noxious qualities of the model species. There are some general conditions to this theory, including 1) the fact that both organisms should occur sympatrically, 2) the mimics should be less able to defend themselves than the models, and 3) that the copied characteristics of the mimic are only external. There are a few others as well.

▶
Probably the most well-known case of mimicry lies in the case of the tri-colored kingsnakes and Milk Snakes (genus *Lampropeltis*) and the coral snakes (genus *Micrurus*). There has even been a popular saying tailored around it: "Red touching yellow can kill a fellow, red touching black, poisons lack."

◀ & ▲
The Banded Rock Rattlesnake, *Crotalus lepidus klauberi*, has long been considered the model for the Nuevo Leon Kingsnake, *Lampropeltis mexicana "thayeri."* For the field worker, however, the latter can be superficially distinguished by a sleeker body and of course the lack of a rattle.

◀ & ▶
Sometimes mimicry can be detrimental to the survival of the mimic in question, especially when human intervention plays a part. The Eastern Milk Snake, *Lampropeltis triangulum triangulum*, (right) for example, is probably not even a true mimic of the Northern Copperhead, *Agkistrodon contortrix mokasen*, (left) but many are mistaken as such and killed on sight.

▶ A strange aspect of the *Lampropeltis/Micrurus* situation in the Americas, however, is the fact that there are more mimics than models, which is not in step with part of the Batesian theory discussed in the opening paragraph.

▲ & ▶
It is unsurprising to learn that in snakes, most mimic models, if not all of them, are venomous, but not all mimics are necessarily completely harmless. The New Guinean Boa, *Candoia aspera*, (also known as the Viper Boa) is certainly capable of causing a human being superficial harm (tearing of skin, extensive bleeding, etc.), but they are certainly not as dangerous as their models, the Northern Death Adders, *Acanthophis antarcticus*.

MODIFICATIONS IN SNAKES

Snakes are, like all living things, subjects of evolution and thus subject to evolve. Through this long, drawn-out process, some snakes have developed interesting morphological modifications which allow them to better survive in their natural environment. By definition, a modification is a change in a creatures currently existing form which, as I said above, helps them better cope with the trials of survival. These modifications can be in color and pattern, dentition (teeth), reproduction, locomotion, or a whole array of other details.

▶

The laterally flattened tail is a modification seen in quite a number of snakes and seems to serve more than one purpose. In sea snakes, for example, it serves as a rudder. In this Red Pipe Snake, *Cylindrophis rufus*, it is used as a defense mechanism, being raised when the snake feels threatened.

▼ Burrowing snakes have an interesting physical modification that almost anyone can recognize—their snouts are usually heavier and the rostral scale reinforced, allowing them to dig better. In the case of the Scarlet Snakes, *Cemophora coccinea*, their snouts are also pointed, a further modification which helps them break through reptile eggs to get to the yolk inside.

◄ The valvular nostrils on a sea snake are an excellent example of morphological modification. These tiny, round organs allow the snake to breath when it surfaces and disallows salt water to enter the respiratory system when they are submerged.

A very large number of snakes have vertical pupils which allow them to see better during the night hours. It thus follows logic that most snakes with these pupils are nocturnal, but that does not always hold true. It is also believed that snakes with vertical pupils have better eyesight in general. ▲

▲ Modifications for defense are very common in snakes since they are basically helpless against predators (except in the case of venomous species of course). The Mud Snakes, *Farancia abacura*, for example, have a brightly colored ventrum (belly) which is effective in scaring off creatures who might be thinking about turning them into meals.

▲ & ▶
Venomous snakes have perhaps the most intense modifications of all—their teeth. Generally speaking, there are three types: rear-fanged, fixed front-fanged, and movable front-fanged. Furthermore, the rattlesnakes have developed an addition to their tails which, when shaken very quickly, creates a buzzing sound. This is simply a warning signal designed to give possible "attackers" a chance to back off before they strike.

KINGSNAKES and MILK SNAKES

There is little doubt that the kingsnakes and the milk snakes, genus *Lampropeltis*, are the most commonly kept snakes of all time. They seem to have it all—looks, temperament, a most remarkable adaptability to captive, and a voracious appetite. There are many, many varieties of *Lampropeltis*, both on the species and subspecies level, although the status of many of the latter always seems to be in question. King and milk snakes have been bred regularly in captivity for many years and are available in a few albino varieties as well.

▲ The Gray-banded Kingsnakes, *Lampropeltis alterna*, are unquestionably among the most popular of all pet snakes. Interestingly, however, they were only described in 1901.

▶ The "nominate" or main subspecies of the Common Kingsnake is the Eastern, or Common, Chain Kingsnake, *Lampropeltis getula getula*. It is a mild-tempered mouse- and snake-eater from the United States Coastal Plains and has been bred repeatedly in captivity.

◄Many king and milk snakes have what are known as "broken patterns," which usually consist of half-saddles or bands—those which are not evenly spaced, etc. This Mexican Milk Snake, *L. t. annulata*, for example, would be perfect if not for the half saddle third from the head.

► The California Kingsnake, *Lampropeltis getula californiae*, has mystified herpetologists for decades. It comes in two complete color and pattern varieties (longitudinally striped or banded, and black or brown with yellow or white), and yet beyond that it is morphologically indistinct.

► Although the Sonoran Mountain Kingsnake, *Lampropeltis pyromelana*, is a beautiful example of a tri-colored kingsnake, its high price and stubborness to eat anything beyond small lizards keep it from being a common pet.

The kingsnakes and the milk snakes only occur in the Americas, but are very widespread in that area. They reach as far north as southern Ontario and Quebec and as far south as Ecuador and Venezuela. They are on both coasts of the United States and can be found in Baja California as well. Since they are so widespread, intergradation occasionally occurs, and this often propels the work of dedicated taxonomists into great turmoil.

The name *Lampropeltis* is Greek for "shiny shield" and probably refers to the reflective and/or smooth quality of the scales of the king and milk snakes.

▶ The Mountain Kingsnake, *Lampropeltis zonata*, is one of the rarer species of the genus. There are currently six accepted subspecies in the group, all of which are rarely seen both on the commercial market and in the wild.

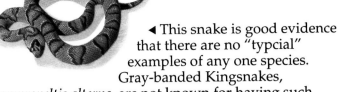

◄ This snake is good evidence that there are no "typcial" examples of any one species. Gray-banded Kingsnakes, *Lampropeltis alterna*, are not known for having such pronounced hazes of yellow in their saddles. But this specimen certainly challenges that rule.

▼ Head closeup of the Sinaloan Milk Snake, *Lampropeltis triangulum sinaloae*.

Not all king or milk snakes are strikingly colored. This Black Kingsnake, *Lampropeltis getula niger*, for example, more resembles the Black Rat Snake, *Elaphe obsoleta obsoleta*, or the Black Pine Snake, *Pituophis melanoleucus lodingi*, than any of the *Lampropeltis* ◄ snakes.

In another example of intergradation, the Eastern Milk Snake, *Lampropeltis triangulum triangulum*, shown here, interbreeds with the well-known Scarlet Kingsnake, *Lampropeltis triangulum elapsoides*, producing what is called the Coastal Plains Milk Snake, *L. t. "temporalis."* ▲

23

RAT SNAKES

Among the most popular of all hobby snakes, the rat snakes are indeed very interesting creatures. The shapes of their bodies have been described, in cross-section, as looking like a "loaf of bread." The bellies are flat, then turn sharply upward, rounding off at the top (the dorsum). The young of rat snakes are attractively patterned with lines, saddles, or bands, but many varieties lose these patterns with age, some becoming uniformly colored, like the Black Rat Snake, *Elaphe obsoleta obsoleta*, for instance. They are hardy captives, taking rats and mice reliably and breeding without much trouble.

For years herpetologists have been under the mistaken impression that the Rosy Rat Snake, *Bogertophis rosaliae*, was named after a woman named Rosy, but the true origin of the moniker lies in the Mexican town of Santa Rosalia.▼

A good example of rat snake patterns that change with age lies with this juvenile Yellow Rat Snake, *Elaphe obsoleta quadrivittata*. Notice the dorsal saddles, which will fade, and the two dorsal stripes, which will become stronger. ▼

▶The reason *Elaphe rufodorsata* is known as the Chinese Garter Snake is that many people consider it to be just that. It has many garter snake qualities, including a liking for frogs and a strong affinity to water.

There are four currently accepted genera of rat snakes, although some taxonomists disagree with this. This *Senticolis triaspis intermedia*, for example, is sometimes placed in the genus *Elaphe*. ▶

One of the most attractive rat snakes is the Trans-Pecos Rat Snake, *Bogertophis subocularis*. Some people still prefer to classify these in *Elaphe*. They are being bred widely in captivity and are now affordably priced. ▼

There is always the possibility of creating taxonomic confusion whenever you refer to a group of animals by a simple common name, and the rat snakes are a good example of this. Most of the rat snakes belong to the genus *Elaphe,* but not all of them do. There is also *Senticolis, Bogertophis,* and *Gonyosoma,* as well. This is one of the dangers of using English common names rather than the more specific Latin ones.

▶   Of the two subspecies of Corn Snake, this one, known as the Great Plains Rat, *Elaphe guttata emoryi,* is not seen as often in the herp hobby although it has all the qualities of its relative, *Elaphe guttata guttata.* It is hardy, even-tempered, and easy to breed.

◀   The Corn Snake, *Elaphe guttata guttata,* is perhaps the most popular rat snake in today's herpetological hobby. It is constantly being bred in captivity, and is available in a number of color, pattern, and albinistic and melanistic varieties.

◄There is a very broad theory which states that snakes with round pupils are more active during the day and those with vertical (catlike) pupils are active during the night. But rat snakes are a good example of an exception. The pupil in this Gray Rat Snake, *Elaphe obsoleta spiloides*, is obviously round, but it can be found moving about both day and night.

▲ Not many rat snakes can claim to be known for a reliably even temperament, but this one can. It is the Mandarin Rat Snake, *Elaphe mandarina*, occurring in the mountain forests of Burma, Vietnam, and China. It has become enormously popular in the hobby of herpetology over the last decade.

Of all the snakes that have been offered for sale in albino varieties, none have been as popular and widely seen as the Corn Snake, *Elaphe guttata guttata*. ▶

BULLSNAKES, PINE SNAKES, and GOPHER SNAKES

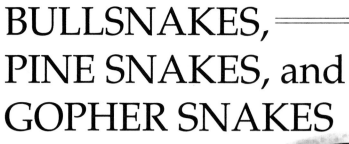

Popular in the hobby and widespread across the United States, Baja, and into northern Mexico, members of the genus *Pituophis* are among the most heavily built snakes in North America. When angered, they will open their mouths just slightly and release a loud, drawn-out hissing sound that slightly resembles that of a tire deflating. However, this action is often a bluff rather than a prelude to attack since the snakes of this genus are relatively peaceful and well mannered.

▲ The Gopher Snakes, *Pituophis catenifer*, were so named because of their habit of living in gopher burrows. Presumably, these snakes would crawl into a gopher hole, turn the occupants into meals, then use the place as a new home.

◄ Gopher Snakes, *Pituophis catenifer*, spend most of their time on the ground, but they will venture into trees and shrubs in search of birds and their eggs.

The head of *Pituophis* is fairly typical of the colubrids, except for the rostral plate (the snout), which is modified for burrowing by being heavier and slightly enlarged. ▶

A striped variant of the Pacific Gopher Snake, *Pituophis catenifer catenifer*, would at one time have been considered a true rarity, but since these have been bred repeatedly in captivity, they no longer hold any real "novelty" value. ▶

▼ The Black Pine Snakes, *Pituophis melanoleucus lodingi*, have fascinated herpetologists for years. As hatchlings they have a full pattern, but as they approach adulthood like the specimen shown here they start to become dark. This is common with some snakes, but unique to this particular subspecies of *Pituophis*.

Mexico only has four members of the *Pituophis* genus. Unfortunately, very little is known about them. Shown here is the Mexican Pine Snake, *Pituophis deppei deppei.*▲

GARTER SNAKES and RIBBON SNAKES

Known for their liveliness and adaptability to captivity, the garter snakes and the ribbon snakes, genus *Thamnophis*, are often the first snakes a junior herpetologist will ever keep. They are commonly sold in the pet shops and will usually be the least expensive serpents in the store. In the wild, *Thamnophis* snakes will rarely stray far from water. Although capable of holding their tempers, they will probably be squirmy and irascible when first picked up. Their bites, however, are hardly what you would call dangerous.

The Checkered Garter Snake, *Thamnophis marcianus marcianus*, has an interesting history. It was discovered during the U.S. military's Louisiana Territory Expedition led by Captain Randolph Barnes Marcy in 1852. ▶

◀ When angered, a garter or ribbon snake may flatten its head and puff out its body. This can be followed by a series of quick bites which, regardless of their small size, can sometimes be quite painful.

Some *Thamnophis* species occur as far north as Canada, which suggests a very high tolerance for cold temperatures. While this may be commonplace for some animals, it is unusual for snakes. ▼

▲ One of the nicest things about keeping garter and ribbon snakes is that they can be maintained on a diet of either earthworms or goldfish. For most keepers, these items are not difficult to supply.

◄ Garter and ribbon snakes are among the most alert and intelligent of all North American colubrids.

Ironically enough, although garter snakes are generally thought of as very common, the San Francisco Garter Snake, *Thamnophis sirtalis tetrataenia*, is one of the rarest snakes in the United States, if not *the* rarest.▼

▲ Garter snakes got their name from their superficial resemblance to the garters used to hold up men's socks. Many believe there is a connection to women's garters as well.

THE BOIDS

Among the most popular of all the hobby snakes are the boids, or, the boas and the pythons. They acquire the name "boids" from the family name—Boidae. By definition, boids are very large snakes (usually over 1 meter) with visible pelvic remnants (anal spurs) and very large teeth. In captivity, they range from simple to almost impossible to keep. Some have very demanding victual requirements and others have such a propensity to biting that they could be considered dangerous. Many species are protected by environmental laws and cannot be obtained by hobbyists. Nevertheless, the boids retain an undeniable mystique and probably always will.

▼ One of the most diverse yet rarely seen boid genera is *Eryx*, otherwise known as the sand boas. These snakes are crepuscular burrowers that prowl around on the surface for lizards and small rodents.

▲
One problem many boid keepers face is dealing with their immense size. Not only does this mean a keeper has to supply his or her animal with plenty of food, but plenty of room as well. In the case of very large specimens, many hobbyists will move beyond glass tanks and actually build their own.

▶ Like many other snakes, certain boid species have colors during their early years that will change later on. This *Liasis boa*, for example, will lose its brilliance in adulthood and appear quite dull.

A few sand boas, genus *Eryx*, are seen for sale in the herp hobby, but since they spend much of their time hiding they do not make very good pets. Many also refuse to feed.
▶

◀ One of the most popular boids is the Ball Python, *Python regius*. At 1.5 meters (average adult length), it is also one of the smallest. It occurs in Western and Central Africa and can be fed on small rodents exclusively. It also has the pleasant reputation of being one of the most even-tempered pythons a keeper could obtain.

The problem with any snakes becoming too popular (and those in the family Boidae are certainly good examples) is that they will also become victims of merciless and shameful exploitation. To illustrate the point, just think of how many thousands of boas and pythons have been hunted down in their native environment, thrown into dark burlap sacks, and shipped to any number of places for future sale. Thus, the need for captive breeding programs presents itself because there are a staggering number of boids that are now so low in population that actual extinction is now a very real threat.

▶
The tree boas, genus *Corallus*, have always been very popular in the herp hobby although they are rather expensive. Some, like the well-known Green Tree Boa, *C. caninus*, can be maintained on a diet of mice and birds, whereas this Garden Tree Boa, *Corallus enydris*, will take a few other things as well.

◀ Some boids use their tails as instruments of defense to frighten off predators. An animal hunting for prey may take this sight as the snake's head and turn away. Such a practice suggests a more passive demeanor than many people imagine snakes to be capable of.

▼ Most people think of boas and pythons as long, gigantic creatures, but there are in fact a number of species that are quite small. This Viper Boa, *Candoia aspera*, for example, will not exceed 1 meter.

▲ The Boa Constrictor, *Boa constrictor*, has always been a highly celebrated boid. It is moderately easy to breed in captivity and gives litters of up to 40 young. Shown is the Hog Island Boa, a somewhat rarely seen variant of the prevalent Common Boa.

▼ The Mexican Burrowing Python, *Loxocemus bicolor*, has a highly developed snout modified for digging, or as its common name implies, burrowing. This shy creature only reveals itself during the night hours or after warm rains.

The sand boas, genus *Eryx*, have a somewhat misleading common name. Only one species, the Desert Boa, *Eryx miliaris*, is truly a "sand" snake. The remainder of the species occur in steppe and rocky regions. The species depicted, *Eryx johnii*, is a resident of dry soil regions. ▶

ALBINISM IN SNAKES

In common terms, albinism is the condition that occurs when the normal (dominant) gene that produces melanin fails to function and the abnormal (recessive) gene acts in its place. A snake will lose all dark coloration and appear as a pinkish animal with some whites and yellows remaining. Albino snakes are very popular in the herp hobby and new varieties appear every year. Some can be very expensive, but are striking in appearance and thus prized by collectors.

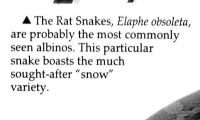

▲ The Rat Snakes, *Elaphe obsoleta*, are probably the most commonly seen albinos. This particular snake boasts the much sought-after "snow" variety.

▼ Albino Gopher Snakes, *Pituophis catenifer*, were at one time considered quite rare, but now they are widely available. They make excellent pets.

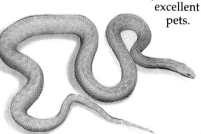

▲
In this photo you can easily see the difference between a normally colored snake (left head) and an albino (right head). Notice the lack of darker colors in the albino, and furthermore the red eyes.

▲ Hybridization between genera made a small wave in herpetoculture at one point, but then seemed to die off. This attractive newborn is the product of an albino Corn Snake and a Sinaloan Milk Snake.

▲ One problem with albino snakes is unpredictable temperament. You may find that an albino snake belonging to an otherwise reputedly "calm" species will have a very nasty disposition.

◀ With so much captive breeding going on, there is the sad but inevitable problem of mixing up albinistic varieties so much that one isn't even sure what he or she is seeing. This Corn Snake, for example, is atypical of the "standard" albino coloring.

FREAKS and MISFITS

Pattern and body mutations are truly a rare phenomenon in the animal world, producing some of the strangest-looking, although occasionally beautiful, creatures ever seen. The generally accepted theory as to why mutations occur states that a gene is attacked by cosmic rays (which are always present all around us) and thus altered from its normal function. Genes are nothing more than proteins made up of complex amino acid compounds. They are fairly fragile, which presents the question as to why mutations don't occur more often.

◄Taking a normally blotched snake and breeding it into a striped one (or vice-versa) has become a bit of a "trend" in modern herpetoculture. This is a young Corn Snake, *Elaphe guttata guttata*, which normally has nut-brown saddles rather than the bacon-red stripes seen here.

◄ Some snakes seem to have no truly reliable "pattern" and thus occur in a number of appearances. This *Sonora aemula*, for example, probably doesn't look like any other of its kind.

Some pattern anomalies present animals which are rather ugly, but others appear rather attrative. The "new" pattern on this Corn Snake, *Elaphe guttata guttata*, for example, is not particularly unsightly. ►

◀ Perhaps the most striking of all developmental flaws is bicephalia, or two-headedness. Most snakes born with two heads do not live beyond infancy, but every now and then a specimen will grow into a healthy adult.

When a pattern is erased by a mutated gene, the area where the pattern would go is usually replaced by the ground (base) color. On this Sinaloan Milk Snake, *Lampropeltis triangulum sinaloae*, the black and white saddles have almost vanished, and the spaces are filled in with rich red. ▶

VENOMOUS SNAKES

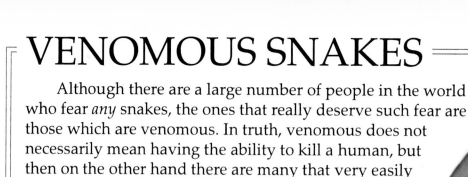

Although there are a large number of people in the world who fear *any* snakes, the ones that really deserve such fear are those which are venomous. In truth, venomous does not necessarily mean having the ability to kill a human, but then on the other hand there are many that very easily could.

Venomous snake species can be found on every continent except Antarctica. In certain countries there are native cults that worship venomous snakes, and the venom itself is used widely for medical purposes. There is also (unfortunately) a rising market for goods made from venomous snakes, including hats, belts, belt buckles, taxidermy mounts, and so on.

▶ Many of the *Trimeresurus* species have become popular in the herp hobby of the last decade. These handsome pit vipers are easy to breed, appear in a wide variety of colors and patterns, are relatively sedate, and their venom is not particularly toxic (although that is not to say they cannot cause human fatalities).

The cobras, *Naja* spp., have probably inspired more fear in the heart of humanity than any other venomous serpent. The infamous hood-spreading display is a very dramatic warning signal and usually precedes a bite that is well-known for its life-stealing quality. ▶

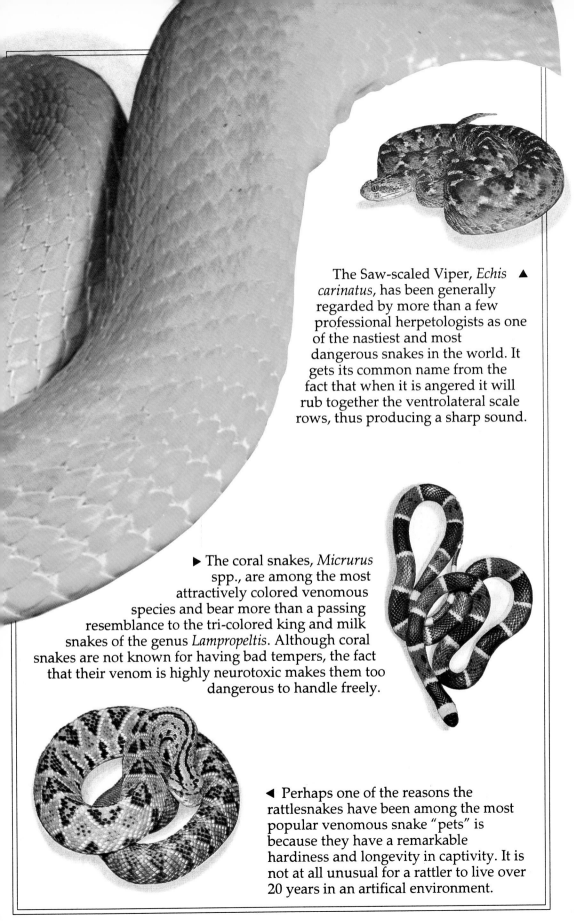

The Saw-scaled Viper, *Echis* ▲ *carinatus*, has been generally regarded by more than a few professional herpetologists as one of the nastiest and most dangerous snakes in the world. It gets its common name from the fact that when it is angered it will rub together the ventrolateral scale rows, thus producing a sharp sound.

▶ The coral snakes, *Micrurus* spp., are among the most attractively colored venomous species and bear more than a passing resemblance to the tri-colored king and milk snakes of the genus *Lampropeltis*. Although coral snakes are not known for having bad tempers, the fact that their venom is highly neurotoxic makes them too dangerous to handle freely.

◀ Perhaps one of the reasons the rattlesnakes have been among the most popular venomous snake "pets" is because they have a remarkable hardiness and longevity in captivity. It is not at all unusual for a rattler to live over 20 years in an artifical environment.

There is a theory that is generally accepted as valid throughout the scientific world which states that snake venoms are nothing more than highly modified forms of saliva. These toxins arose when the early legless reptiles had to develop some way of subduing their prey. Some became constrictors, some simply relied on their powerful jaws to crush their items to death, and others developed fangs in which to channel their toxic saliva from the glandular sacs located in their upper jaw just below and behind their eyes.

▶ Sea snakes are rarely seen in captivity outside zoos and aquariums. Perhaps this is best since their captive requirements are virtually impossible for the average keeper to provide, not to mention the fact that their venom is the most potent of all snake poisons.

▲ Wagler's Pit Viper, *Trimeresurus wagleri*, is one of the most attractive snakes in the world, as you can tell by looking at the beautiful specimens on this branch. They appear in a variety of colors and patterns, this one being known to some as the "Kalimantan" phase.

It is considered unusual for a rattlesnake to have any more than six or seven segments on its tail at any one time, but occasionally such things happen. The *Crotalus tortugensis* shown here has 15.▶

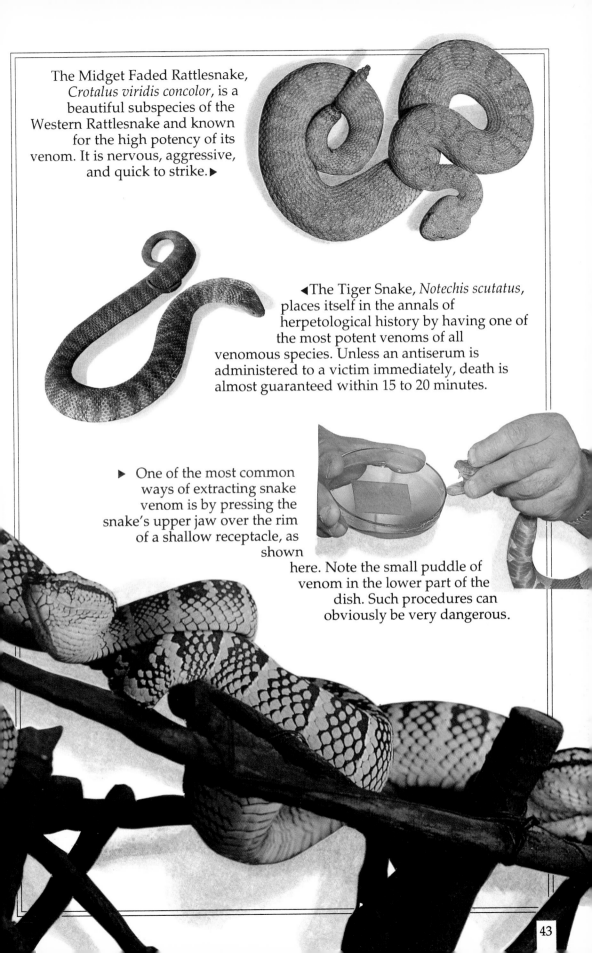

The Midget Faded Rattlesnake, *Crotalus viridis concolor*, is a beautiful subspecies of the Western Rattlesnake and known for the high potency of its venom. It is nervous, aggressive, and quick to strike. ▶

◀The Tiger Snake, *Notechis scutatus*, places itself in the annals of herpetological history by having one of the most potent venoms of all venomous species. Unless an antiserum is administered to a victim immediately, death is almost guaranteed within 15 to 20 minutes.

▶ One of the most common ways of extracting snake venom is by pressing the snake's upper jaw over the rim of a shallow receptacle, as shown here. Note the small puddle of venom in the lower part of the dish. Such procedures can obviously be very dangerous.

REAR-FANGED SNAKES

"Opisthoglyphous" is probably not a word most herpetoculturists use in their everyday speech, but it nevertheless applies to a great number of snakes that have been kept in terrariums for years (the Hognose Snakes, genus *Heterodon*, for example). Opisthoglyphous means rear-fanged and refers to those species that have fangs located not in the front of the mouth, as in solenoglyphs (snakes with movable front fangs) or proteroglyphs (snakes with fixed front fangs), but instead in the back. Most rear-fanged snakes are harmless enough, but some can cause skin reactions and two are known to regularly cause human deaths.

▶
The
Cat-eyed
Snakes, genus
Leptodeira, are calm,
attractive serpents that
occur mainly in the tropics,
just reaching into southern
Texas. They are nocturnal
and terrestrial and feed
mainly on frogs and toads
but have been known to
take lizards and the
occasional mouse. Their
bites are not serious (and
they do not bite often) and
some have survived for
over 20 years in captivity.

The Vine Snakes, genus *Oxybelis*, attain
their common name from their resemblance
to vines, which many people have mistaken
them for. They spend most of their time in trees and
shrubs and their bodily colors usually blend in well
with their background. They occur mostly in the
tropics but touch into extreme southern Arizona as
well. ▼

▲ A resident of tropical
American rainforest regions,
members of the genus *Oxyrhopus* are
very colorful, some bearing a striking
resemblance to the coral snakes of the genus
Micrurus and *Micruroides*. Their bites, while not
particularly painful, can pose potential danger to humans
through swelling, burning, and mild tissue damage.

▲
Superficially,
some rear-fanged snakes hold more than a passing resemblance to many non-fanged (aglyphous) species. This *Psammophis jallae*, for example, could easily be mistaken for a whipsnake, genus *Masticophis*. Such mistakes could be costly; *Psammophis* has a nasty bite and one or two species can cause harsh illnesses.

Although subfamilies are regarded by some taxonomists as superficial at best and hardly worth recognizing, it should be noted that the subfamily Boiginae was designed specifically to house most of the rear-fanged snakes. It is part of the Colubridae, which is the largest of all snake families.

▶

◀ There are quite a number of "harmless" rear-fanged snake genera that occur in the United States (there are no harmful ones), and most of those are found in the drier desert regions of the West. The ground snakes, *Sonora* spp., can be found over much of this area. Snakes of this genus are small, secretive burrowers that feed largely on small invertebrates.

The Herald Snake, *Crotaphopeltis hotamboeia*, is a hardy snake with a large range; it can be found over the entire southern half of Africa. It rarely strays far from damp areas and hides in snatches of dense vegetation where it waits for unsuspecting frogs to hop by. ▼

▲ Snakes of the genus *Telescopus* are odd examples of the opisthoglyphs. Victims of their bites have reported very severe reactions, but there have been no known fatalities. This suggests that their venom is highly developed and, through evolution, may eventually become deadly.

TREE-DWELLING SPECIES

The term "arboreal" means "tree-dwelling" and applies to a great number of snake species. The bodies of these snakes have been highly modified through the ages specifically for survival in such places. The many boids which live in trees, for example, have special muscular structures which allow them to comfortably wrap around the hard surface of a tree branch or move and climb from place to place when necessary. It is also unsurprising to learn that most of the foods arboreal snakes eat are arboreal themselves. Items include birds and bats as well as any small mammals that will venture off the ground for whatever reason, plus some insects too.

◄
The prehensile tail is virtually always present on arboreal snakes. It serves as an anchor for many of their activities, including sleeping, in some cases breeding, and to keep them in place when they lash out at prey items. Shown here is the graceful Yellow-lined Palm Viper, *Bothrops lateralis*, from the cloud-forest regions of Panama and Costa Rica.

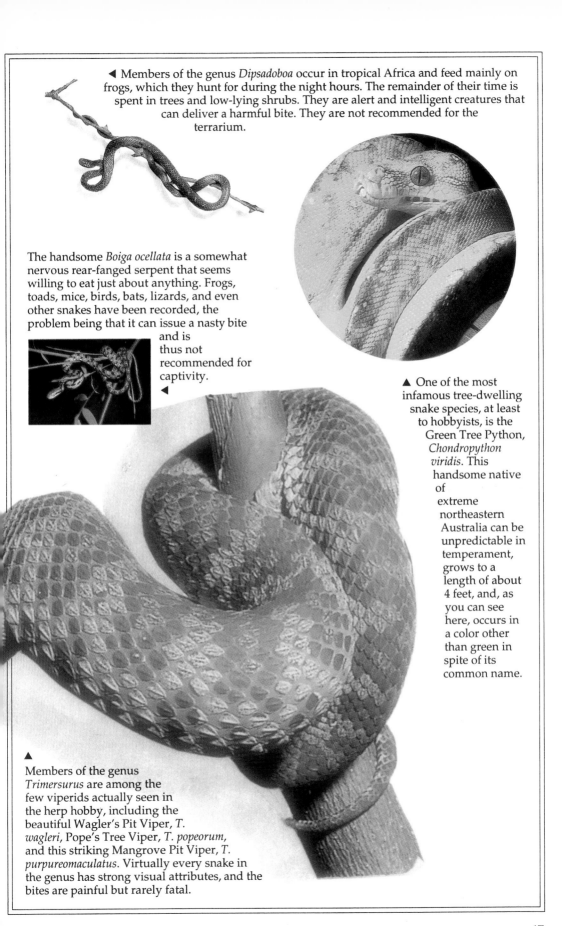

◀ Members of the genus *Dipsadoboa* occur in tropical Africa and feed mainly on frogs, which they hunt for during the night hours. The remainder of their time is spent in trees and low-lying shrubs. They are alert and intelligent creatures that can deliver a harmful bite. They are not recommended for the terrarium.

The handsome *Boiga ocellata* is a somewhat nervous rear-fanged serpent that seems willing to eat just about anything. Frogs, toads, mice, birds, bats, lizards, and even other snakes have been recorded, the problem being that it can issue a nasty bite and is thus not recommended for captivity. ◀

▲ One of the most infamous tree-dwelling snake species, at least to hobbyists, is the Green Tree Python, *Chondropython viridis*. This handsome native of extreme northeastern Australia can be unpredictable in temperament, grows to a length of about 4 feet, and, as you can see here, occurs in a color other than green in spite of its common name.

▲
Members of the genus *Trimersurus* are among the few viperids actually seen in the herp hobby, including the beautiful Wagler's Pit Viper, *T. wagleri*, Pope's Tree Viper, *T. popeorum*, and this striking Mangrove Pit Viper, *T. purpureomaculatus*. Virtually every snake in the genus has strong visual attributes, and the bites are painful but rarely fatal.

SNAKES OF NORTH AMERICA

The continent of North America, which naturally includes Canada, is home to some of the most iteresting herpetofauna in the world. Natural habitats include rough, rocky mountains, hot, silent deserts, flat plains, pine woodlands, and thick, mucky swamps. Most North American snake genera belong to the family Colubridae, but there are also two in the family Boidae, three in Viperidae, and two, the Coral Snakes, the genera *Micrurus* and *Micruroides*, in Elapidae, which makes them relatives of the deadly cobras.

◀ Rarely seen in the hobby, and for that matter in the wild, the Sonoran Shovel-nosed Snake is nevertheless a fascinating creature. It occurs in mesquite and creosote regions of southern Arizona and eats a variety of small invertebrates (although some captives may refuse food entirely).

▲ The green snakes, genus *Opheodrys*, have always been immensely popular with beginning hobbyists. They are mild-tempered and can be kept alive on a diet that usually consists of nothing but crickets. And, contrary to popular belief, they are not only easy to breed, but the young are not difficult to care for either.

The Coachwhips, *Masticophis flagellum*, may be sleek, attractive, and willing to eat in captivity, but their notoriety for nastiness is probably the one factor that has kept them from commercial popularity. A further detail to this reputation is their tendency to aim for one's face. ▼

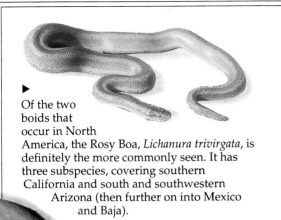

▶ Of the two boids that occur in North America, the Rosy Boa, *Lichanura trivirgata*, is definitely the more commonly seen. It has three subspecies, covering southern California and south and southwestern Arizona (then further on into Mexico and Baja).

▶ The Eastern Indigo Snake, *Drymarchon corais couperi*, is one of the rarest and most controversial snakes in North America. It was common up until the mid-1970's when systematic gassing of tortoise burrows greatly reduced its numbers.

The kingsnakes, of the genus *Lampropeltis*, are well-known throughout the herpetocultural hobby. There are eight species in the genus (those in *L. triangulum* being known as the milk snakes), most of which are currently being bred and raised in captivity. They are attractive and generally very docile. ▼

The Scarlet Snake, *Cemophora coccinea*, is one of the most fascinating yet easily overlooked snakes in North America. It occurs exclusively in the eastern and southeastern United States (down into southern Texas) and can only be found prowling about during the night hours. It is a veteran burrower that feeds almost entirely on reptile eggs. ▼

▲ A rarely seen snake with an interesting natural history is the Leafnose Snake, genus *Phyllorynchus*. There are two species, *P. browni* and *P. decurtatus*, both of which will gladly feed on lizards and their eggs. Their name was obviously garnered from the shape of their enlarged rostral scale.

SNAKES OF CENTRAL AND SOUTH AMERICA

South and Central America are known collectively in zoogeographical terms as the "neotropical" region. The neotropics probably have the highest diversity of living things on earth. Everything from long stretches of silent desert to thick snatches of shimmering rainforest are incorporated into this unique natural communtiy, so it is no surprise that a large number of snake species occur there are well. Such a variety of environments makes South and Central America an inviting locale for cold-blooded creatures like the snakes, and it's more than likely there are many species not yet accounted for.

This animal's resemblance to the coral snakes, genus *Micurus*, is more than a passing one. In fact, all of the snakes in *Erythrolamprus* are known as "false coral snakes" although they do not possess any of the coral snakes's deadly qualities. They occur in upper Venezuela, Colombia, and into Costa Rica among other places, favoring quiet, terrestrial habitats—piles of leaf litter, decaying logs, and so on. ▼

▲ The Gray-banded Kingsnake, *Lampropeltis alterna*, is well-known throughout the hobby as one of the most popular snakes of all time. It can be found prowling about the roads at night in a few areas of Mexico (and into western Texas) and is now known to be much more common than originally thought.

There is a remarkably large number of rattlesnakes occurring in Central America, most notably in the Mexican region. The Lance-headed Rattler, *Crotalus polystictus*, shown here, is a native of rocky grasslands, mesquite shrub, and lowland pine forests. It has a notable adaptivity to captive life and can be maintained on a diet of mice. ▼

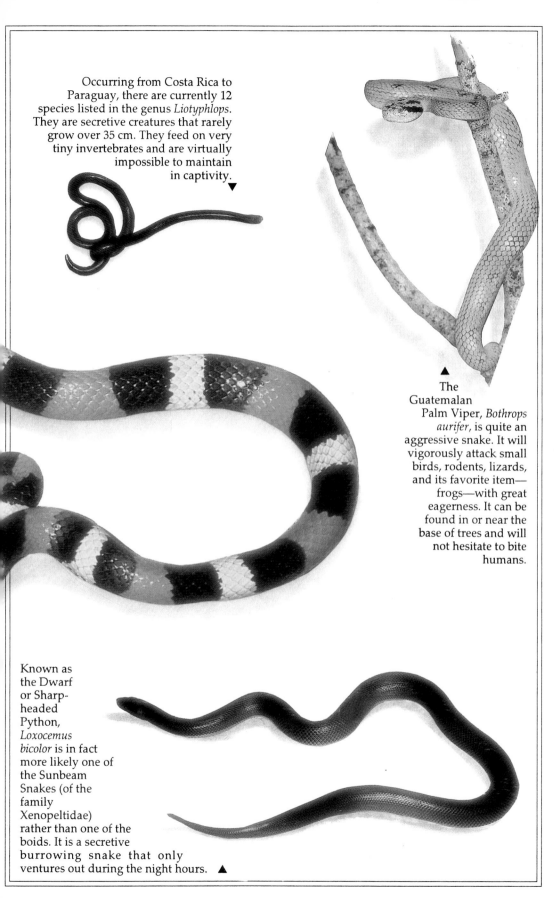

Occurring from Costa Rica to Paraguay, there are currently 12 species listed in the genus *Liotyphlops*. They are secretive creatures that rarely grow over 35 cm. They feed on very tiny invertebrates and are virtually impossible to maintain in captivity. ▼

▲
The Guatemalan Palm Viper, *Bothrops aurifer*, is quite an aggressive snake. It will vigorously attack small birds, rodents, lizards, and its favorite item—frogs—with great eagerness. It can be found in or near the base of trees and will not hesitate to bite humans.

Known as the Dwarf or Sharp-headed Python, *Loxocemus bicolor* is in fact more likely one of the Sunbeam Snakes (of the family Xenopeltidae) rather than one of the boids. It is a secretive burrowing snake that only ventures out during the night hours. ▲

SNAKES OF AFRICA

At present, it is believed that approximately 130 snake species occur in Africa. Of those 130, 35 are fanged, and 14 have proven themselves deadly to humans. In fact, some of the deadliest snakes in the world occur in Africa, including a few species of cobra, two mambas (green and black), the only two deadly rear-fanged snakes (the Boomslang and the African Twig Snake), the infamous Gaboon Viper,

▲

The egg-eating snakes, genus *Dasypeltis*, are indeed fascinating creatures. They can stretch their mouths over eggs much larger than the size of their heads. They will then puncture the egg, and finally consume the yolk and regurgitate the remaining shell.

and a few others. Africa is also home to the families Typhlopidae (Blind Snakes) and Leptotyphlopidae (Thread Snakes), which are tiny little worm-like creatures whose life histories are very poorly known.

The house snakes, genus *Lamprophis*, have made a small but notable stir in the herpetocultural hobby. They are relatively manageable in size (about 80 cm) and feed on rodents and other small vertebrates although some specimens may prefer snakes. This specimen is known as the Olive House Snake, *Lamprophis inornatus*. ▲

The popular Ball Python, *Python regius*, is well-known throughout the herp hobby as being one of the most reliable and even-tempered boids. Many keepers remember this snake as one of their first, and it gets its name from its habit of curling up into a ball when it feels threatened. ▼

A rarely seen burrower, *Amblyodipsas ventrimaculata* is also known as the Kalahari Purple-glossed Snake. It gets its vernacular from the shiny purple coloring on its back. It feeds mainly on small sand-dwelling reptiles and is oviparous, meaning it lays eggs rather than gives live birth. ◄

Residents of Madagascar, the three species of the genus *Langaha* are among the most bizarre-looking members of the order Serpentes. Their vernacular name, the Leafnose Snakes, comes from the appearance of the protruding appendage seen here. Generally speaking, the tips of the males' snouts are sharper than the females'. ▲

SNAKES OF ASIA

Asia is, as most people know, and very large continent, and made up of two main zoogeographic sections—Palearctic and Oriental. The former is part of the Holarctic and defined by having an enormous variety of vegetation, including taiga, deciduous and mixed forest, tundra, steppe, and barren desert. Palearctic regions have clearly defined seasons that are puncuated by changes in temperature (as opposed to more tropical regions which depend on precipitation to draw these boundaries). The Oriental region is delineated from the Palearctic at the southern slopes of the Himalayas and the seasonal differences in this sector are decided by monsoons. The life history of most Asian snakes is poorly known and they rarely appear in the hobby. There is also a large number of venomous species in Asia, many of them deadly.

◀ Another Asian rear-fanged snake, *Psammophis leithi* makes a poor captive. It needs to be kept in a very large terrarium because it likes to move around a lot (the common name for this genus is "sand racers") and even then it may not accept its normal menu of lizards and occasional small rodents.

▶

The cat snake *Telescopus fallax* can be easily recognized by the vertical pupil that gives it its common name. Resembling North and Central America's cat-eyed snakes, genus *Leptodeira*, they are also rear-fanged and can deliver potentially harmful bites.

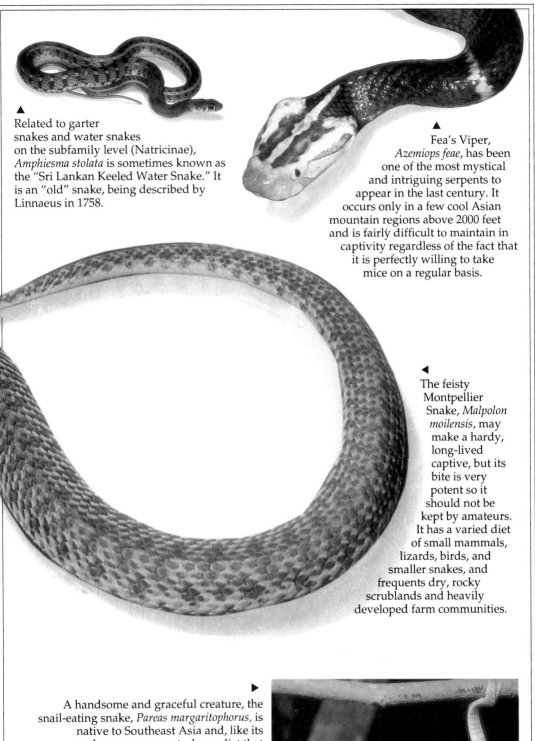

▲
Related to garter snakes and water snakes on the subfamily level (Natricinae), *Amphiesma stolata* is sometimes known as the "Sri Lankan Keeled Water Snake." It is an "old" snake, being described by Linnaeus in 1758.

▲
Fea's Viper, *Azemiops feae*, has been one of the most mystical and intriguing serpents to appear in the last century. It occurs only in a few cool Asian mountain regions above 2000 feet and is fairly difficult to maintain in captivity regardless of the fact that it is perfectly willing to take mice on a regular basis.

◄
The feisty Montpellier Snake, *Malpolon moilensis*, may make a hardy, long-lived captive, but its bite is very potent so it should not be kept by amateurs. It has a varied diet of small mammals, lizards, birds, and smaller snakes, and frequents dry, rocky scrublands and heavily developed farm communities.

▶
A handsome and graceful creature, the snail-eating snake, *Pareas margaritophorus*, is native to Southeast Asia and, like its vernacular name suggests, has a diet that consists almost entirely of snails; land snails to be exact. It can been found in high elevation regions at cool temperatures and is an egglayer.

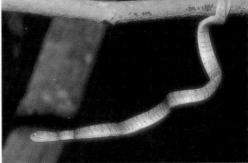

SNAKES OF AUSTRALIA

The main claim to fame the ophidiofauna of Australia has is the largest percentage of venomous species of any continent in the world. Most of them belong to the family Elapidae, including the Death Adder, the highly venomous Tiger Snake, the Taipan, and the oddly named Bandy-bandy. Eight species of sea snake occur in Australian waters and only nine species in the family Colubridae. Most of the terrain in Australia is open and arid, and due to developmental growth, more and more cases of venomous species appearing on public roads or in people's backyards are being reported every year.

▲
Members of the genus *Unechis* are small (around 50 cm), nocturnal creatures that feed exclusively on lizards. They make fairly uninteresting terrarium subjects and their relation to cobras makes them dangerous as well. They are endemic to Australia.

Although known as the "Australian Copperheads" in common English, members of the genus *Austrelaps* are actually in the family Elapidae, taxonomic home to the coral snakes, mambas, and cobras. They are highly dangerous creatures, having caused many deaths, and feed almost exclusively on frogs. ▼

Instantly recognizable by many hobbyists, the Green Tree Python, *Chondropython viridis*, has been a keeper's favorite for many years. Its geographic range just barely reaches into Australia (Cape York, in the extreme Northeast) where it can be found arboreally in any of the remaining rainforest regions. ▶

◀ This magnificent animal is known as the Black-headed Python, *Aspidites melanocephalus*, (the species name means "black head") and is, like so many other Australian snakes, found only on that continent. It has only recently been recognized in the hobby but is becoming popular very quickly.

Stokes's Sea Snake, *Astrotia stokesii*, can be reliably found in Australian waters, then west through Indo-Malayan areas and further on into Sri Lanka. ◀

New Guinean Boa (also known as the Viper Boa), *Candoia aspera*, is occasionally seen in the herp hobby. It will breed in captivity quite willingly provided it has the proper climatic stimuli and can be maintained on a diet of small mammals, frogs, or birds. ▼

SNAKES AND ART

Just as snakes have inspired much folklore and mysticism, so have they inspired much in the way of artwork. For centuries people have used snakes as vehicles of expression, although admittedly most of these expressions were negative ones. Today, snakes are the focus of many photographers (literally), artists, and, sadly, many novelty and clothing manufacturers. People have only recently begun to realize the enormous visual impact snakes have, particularly when set against their natural environments. One strong attribute snakes have going for them is a great variety of colors. Even people who find snakes revolting cannot deny that some species are very beautiful.

Artistic license has, of course, always existed in one form or another, and this drawing from centuries past is evidence of that. The only place where winged snakes ever existed was in the mind of the artist who drew this.
▶

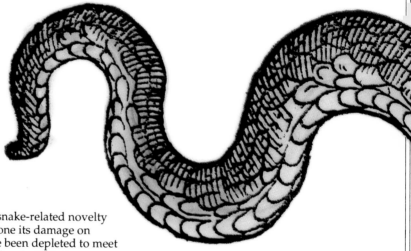

The growing call for snake-related novelty items has of course done its damage on populations that have been depleted to meet the need for skins and so forth, but some manufacturers are decent enough to make their products from ordinary materials. ▼

▲ Since most engravings were done with live models and created so long ago, they tell us much about the history of their subject. Here we learn that snake charmers are truly a long-lived fraternity and thus their particular "talent" has probably become highly developed over the years.

As far as the novelty craze for snake-related items goes, rattlesnakes are probably exploited most often. Sometimes the rattlers will be portrayed harmlessly on a belt buckle like this one, other times the buckle may be made from the skin of an actual snake. ▶

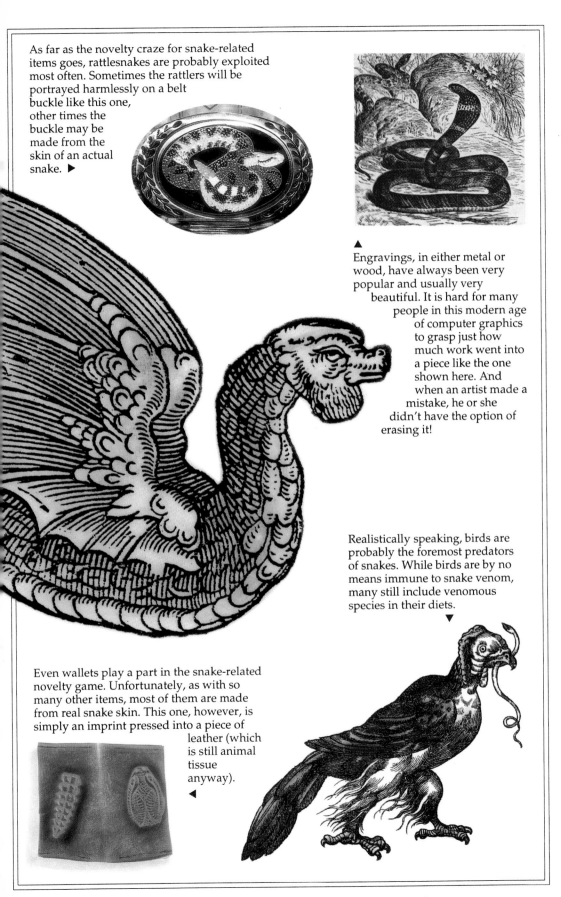

▲
Engravings, in either metal or wood, have always been very popular and usually very beautiful. It is hard for many people in this modern age of computer graphics to grasp just how much work went into a piece like the one shown here. And when an artist made a mistake, he or she didn't have the option of erasing it!

Realistically speaking, birds are probably the foremost predators of snakes. While birds are by no means immune to snake venom, many still include venomous species in their diets.
▼

Even wallets play a part in the snake-related novelty game. Unfortunately, as with so many other items, most of them are made from real snake skin. This one, however, is simply an imprint pressed into a piece of leather (which is still animal tissue anyway).
◀

The wonderful thing about art in any form is that it can be expressed in so many different ways. One need not be able to simply draw a snake to be able to created snake art. There is sculpting, wood carving, and silk-screening; even fine books can be considered art in a way. A number of private firms have begun offering herpetological artwork with the same regard normally given to fine paintings and prints.

▶
For the hobbyist who might want to consider a relaxing sideline to herpetoculture, you can obtain uniform snake castings like this one, then garner a photo of the animal and paint in the colors as accurately as possible. For something like a venomous snake, it may be the closest you may ever come to owning a real one!

▼ Even today, snake-related wood engravings continue to hold a small place in the herp art market. A decorative little piece like this one would be a colorful addition to a herper's snake room, den, or for that matter anywhere else in the home.

▲
It would
probably be
more accurate to say
this is a wood "burned" item
rather then "engraved." The main
instrument used is small wood-
burning "pen" applied to a sketch
made on the wood surface. The
piece is then painted in the
appropriate colors, and the result
is what you see here.

▶
For many years,
old drawings and
engravings like
the one shown
here were the
only visual
records in
existence of
many species,
and therefore the
artist had a great
responsibility to
accuracy. It goes
without saying that
many of these pieces are still perfectly usable today.

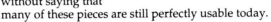

◀
Having living
models to work
from is not
always
possible, especially in cases like this
where the animals depicted obviously
would never sit still for such an
extended period of time. This is truly a
monument to the artist's memory for
detail.

An occasional problem with many of the
older snake drawings is that the artist
either didn't bother to record what species
he or she was using as a model, or, even
worse, the record of
such was wrong. This
can cause much
confusion later if
someone wishes to
identify the animal.
◀

MYTHOLOGY AND FOLKLORE

There is little doubt that snakes have always had a profound emotional impact on humans. Sometimes the reactions have been negative, sometimes positive, but always interesting, and through them many myths and folktales have arisen. It is always fascinating and even amusing to hear what tall stories a backwoodsman can tell concerning his last encounter with an angry rattler, or watch a television program on how people of primitive lands regard the snakes of their region. Many venomous species have become the focus of worship and intrigue, when in fact the snakes are often as confused about the attention they are given as we in the "modern world" are!

▶ Rattlesnakes have always been the target of one bizarre perspective or another, and some of those perspectives have caused their populations great harm. The famous "rattlesnake roundups" of North American have done more damage to their numbers than any natural phenomenon. Most rattlers are, in fact, quite shy and would just as soon be left to themselves.

◀ An "enlightened" herpetologist should always be understanding of some of the strange mystiques surrounding snakes, but sometimes this just isn't possible. The Milk Snakes, *Lampropeltis triangulum*, for example, have been given their vernacular from the belief that they suck milk from cows. Knowing that they have no movable lips or affinity to milk, one can easily judge the rationality of such a claim.

The whipsnakes, of the genus *Masticophis*, have really earned a bad reputation over the years. There is a legend that states these quick-moving serpents will actually chase down and "whip people to death" with their tails, when in fact they do nothing of the sort. To be fair, however, they are generally very nervous snakes and thus somewhat nasty.
▶

▲ Cobras are perhaps the most "worshipped" snakes of all time. Centuries ago, natives who lived in close quarters with cobras learned to fear and respect them (which is not surprising for a snake that can kill a human so easily) and thus the deadly snakes found themselves the hub of a multitude of religious cults.

The Rainbow Snake, *Farancia erytrogramma*, has an interesting little myth attached to it. Supposedly the tip of its tail is actually a "stinger" and can produce a touch as painful as that of a bee or a scorpion. In fact, the tail is quite pointed, but not at all dangerous.
▼

◀
The vipers have always had a role in snake mythology and folklore. There are temple vipers in Malaysia that are allowed to roam freely from structure to structure, and others that are believed to possess medicinal qualities rather than destructive ones. And then of course there is the classic tale of Cleopatra, who committed suicide by encouraging the bite of an asp.

INDEX